LOOK & FIND IN THE OCEAN

CLEVER Publishing

Find the orange coral.
Point to the eels.
Find the smallest octopus.
How many sea stars can you count?

Where is the pink squid?
Which sea jelly has the longest tentacles?
Point to all of the shells with red and orange stripes.

Where is the mermaid holding books?
Find the mermaid drinking from a straw.
Can you find the baby?

Point to the merboy wearing yellow sunglasses.
Do you see the mermaid with blue hair?
How many merboys have black hair?

Count the fish with red and yellow stripes.
Can you find the shark with a flower in its mouth?
Point to the narwhals.

Can you find the shark wearing a crown?
Can you find the whale that's upside down?
Point to the shark with its mouth open.

Can you find the crab holding a leaf?
Do you see the turtle with a flower on its head?
Which lobster is the biggest?
Where is the sea snake?

Point to the hermit crab wearing glasses.
How many red sea stars do you count?
Which crab is wearing a hat and necklace?

Where are the purple flip-flops?
Find the girl with the heart-shaped sunglasses.
What colors do you see on the beach ball?
How many pink and orange fish can you find?

Find all of the swimmers wearing goggles.
Point to the float that looks like a watermelon.

Find the diver with the pink flippers.
Point to the smallest boat.
Which diver is wearing an orange wet suit?
How many sailboats do you see?

Find the biggest submarine.
Point to the red buoy.
Which boat has the most life preservers?

How many blue gemstones can you count?
Find the shell necklace.
Find the treasure chest that's closed.
Where is the smallest crab?

Which sword is stuck in the sand?
How many clamshells with pearls do you see?
Point to the sea creature wearing an eye patch.

Can you find the fish with black-and-white fins?
Count the blue coral.
Where is the large red fish?
Find the key.

Can you find the clownfish that's hiding?
Point to the green fish.
Find all of the fish that have blue around their eyes.

Find the seal wearing a necklace.
Point to the tent.
Which penguin is wearing a red scarf?

Do you see the seagull on top of an iceberg?
Where is the red flag?
Can you find the penguin wearing a yellow hat?

Find the walrus with its eyes closed.
How many people are ice fishing?
Do you see the bucket with a fish in it?
Which polar bear cub is hiding?